HAL LEONARD
GUITAR METHOD
Supplement to Any Guitar Method

RHYTHM RIFFS
BY GREG KOCH

The accompanying audio was recorded by Greg Koch using a Fender Custom Shop Telecaster® guitar and Fender Cyber Deluxe amp. For more information on Greg Koch go to www.gregkoch.com

To access audio visit:
www.halleonard.com/mylibrary

Enter Code
1561-5612-7903-9282

ISBN 978-0-634-04848-7

HAL•LEONARD®
CORPORATION
7777 W. BLUEMOUND RD. P.O. BOX 13819 MILWAUKEE, WI 53213

In Australia Contact:
Hal Leonard Australia Pty. Ltd.
22 Taunton Drive P.O. Box 5130
Cheltenham East, 3192 Victoria, Australia
Email: ausadmin@halleonard.com

Visit Hal Leonard Online at
www.halleonard.com

INTRODUCTION

Do you find yourself reaching for the same chord shapes again and again when you pick up a guitar? What if someone asks you to "play something bluesy" on a G chord—do you know what to do? How would you like to spice up your rhythm guitar playing, make your parts more authentic, or maybe just get some new ideas?

Rhythm Riffs is a unique book designed for the intermediate to advanced guitarist to increase your playing vocabulary exponentially. Whether you're playing in a band, writing songs, accompanying others, or just jamming with friends, there's so much more you can do—other than strum!—when playing rhythm guitar.

ABOUT THE RIFFS

What is a "riff?" A *riff* is a rhythmic theme that can contain single notes or chords. What goes into a riff can really depend on the style of music or even the particular player. A riff can include any of these elements:

- unique chord voicing(s)
- distinctive rhythm(s)
- hammer-ons/pull-offs
- fills & ornaments
- passing tones & chords
- unusual playing techniques
- other embellishments

The possibilities are nearly endless!

When it comes right down to it, most songs are the same. That is, they're all based on chords. What makes one song—or style, or artist—different from another, is what they do with those chords. This is where *Rhythm Riffs* comes in.

Each riff in this book is based on a simple chord—like A, Em, G7, etc. The chord label doesn't necessarily reflect the actual voicing used; it just shows you what type of chord you may want to play the riff over. This means you can start "plugging in" the riffs right away—putting them into songs, grooves, jams, whatever.

But here's where things get really interesting: Each riff isn't just played once. Instead, through various stylistic nuances, each riff is "morphed" into five different genres of music: rock, blues, jazz, country, and funk.* This gives you an option for just about any style you could possibly play! With twelve major riffs, twelve minor riffs, and twelve dominant seventh riffs, plus the five stylistic variations for each, you've got 180 potential riffs for bolstering your rhythm guitar vocabulary.

The last section of the book features eight variations on the 12-bar blues, also done in various styles, which provide interesting rhythmic ideas and chord voicings for this most popular and highly used song form.

*Folk, R&B, and pop are occasional alternate styles.

HOW TO USE THIS BOOK

There is no right or wrong way to use this book. Some players may want to play each riff in its entirety; others will want to pick and choose just a few chord voicings or techniques out of various riffs. Some players may want to focus on one particular style and learn only those riffs. The option is always yours.

If you started the book at the beginning, it would take you quite a while to get to some of the ideas at the end. Therefore, you may want to "preview" the book first: Listen to the audio while following along with the book, and keep track of the selections that you like. Make those your first playing priority. Each riff is played twice (fast, then slow.) Track 45 contains tuning notes.

HOW TO PRACTICE

When learning the riff selections, practice them along at a speed at which you can play flawlessly. If you try to play them fast too soon, the "slop factor" can be too great. (Always give yourself plenty of time to learn each riff; there's a lot of them here and the tendency may be to rush, but each riff is worth taking your time with.) Using a metronome is very helpful for gradually speeding up pieces that you are trying to learn. Start at a reasonable tempo, and as your skill dictates, increase the tempo.

When trying to apply the riffs, some incubation time is again a good idea. It may help you to have certain tunes in mind—perhaps a song for which you're having trouble finding fresh rhythm ideas. You can try the riffs at your next band rehearsal, record them as you play a tune to see how they sound, play along with records, or whatever it takes to feel conversant with them. Never force a riff, though; strive to make your playing musical. When something works, you'll know it.

The 12-bar variations at the end of the book can be used in their entirety or can be cross-mutated by joining some of the different variations together. The idea is to give you a strong rhythmic vocabulary for comping a blues in any genre.

SPECIAL TECHNIQUES

There are two specialized (right-hand) techniques used in this book on occasion—most often in the country-style riffs—that may require a little explaining before we proceed. One is Travis-style picking, and the other is chicken pickin'.

The *Travis-style* selections in this book are written as two parts like the example below. The lower part can be played with the thumb, while the higher register can be played with the first and second fingers. A hybrid picking ("pick & fingers") approach may also be employed by playing the lower register with your pick while your middle and ring fingers catch the other notes. In either case, muting the lower notes with the palm of your picking hand gives the desired rhythmic approach for this style.

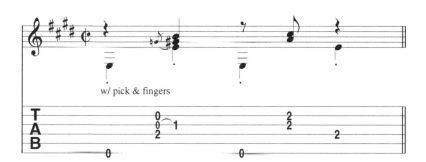

Chicken pickin' means different things to different people, but it basically involves using muting of one form or another to achieve a "clucking"-type sound indicative of a lot of great country guitarists. The muting used to produce chicken pickin', as it occurs in this book, can best be explained with the example below. The three notes of the first A chord are simultaneously plucked by the index, middle, and ring fingers. These same fingers are immediately used to dampen the strings, and the thumb is used to pluck the open A string (which is being muted by the index finger) to produce the "cluck." By rapidly going back and forth between the open chord and the muffled "cluck," your chicken pickin' sequence begins to take shape.

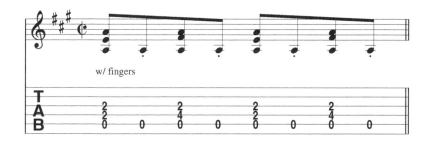

RIFF 1

TRACK 1

ROCK

w/ dist.

R&B

JAZZ

Amaj9

COUNTRY

FUNK

Aadd9

P.M. - - - - -

RIFF 2

TRACK 2

 **RIFF 3**

TRACK 3

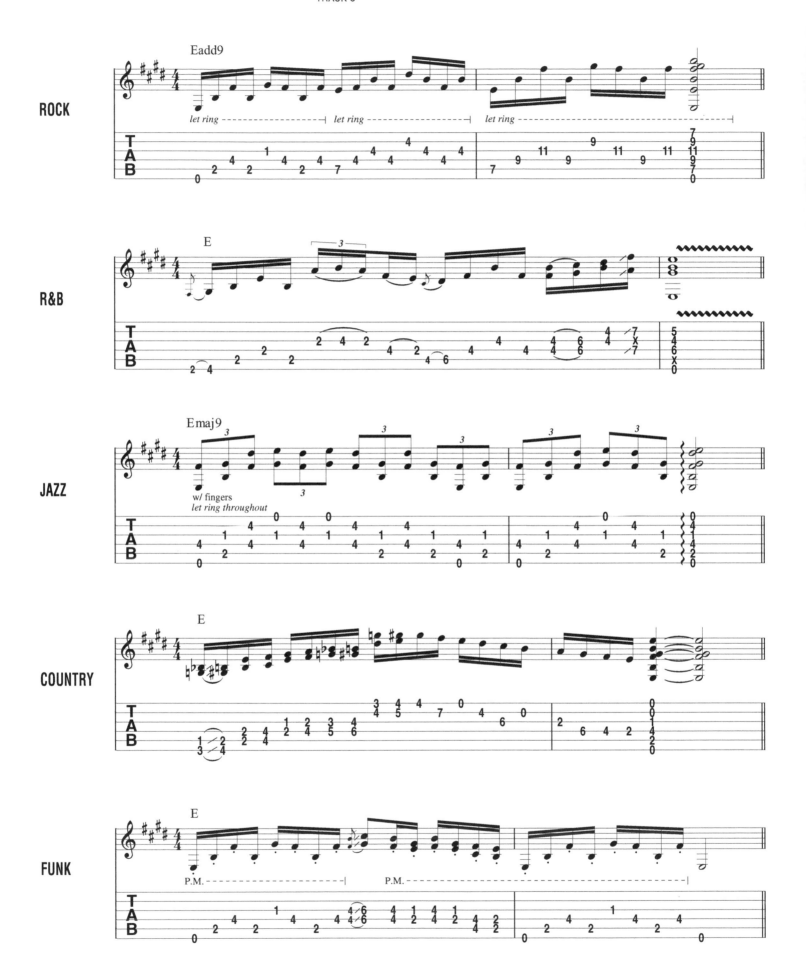

 **RIFF 4**
TRACK 4

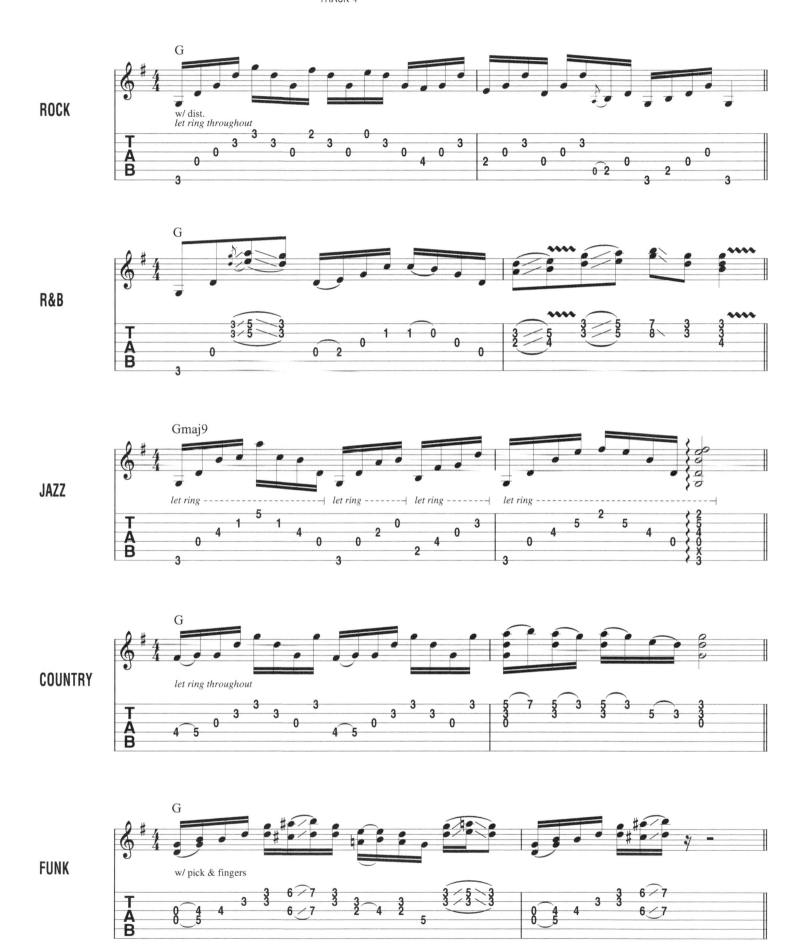

ROCK

R&B

JAZZ

COUNTRY

FUNK

 **RIFF 5**
TRACK 5

RIFF 6

FOLK/ROCK

R&B

JAZZ

COUNTRY

FUNK

RIFF 7

TRACK 7

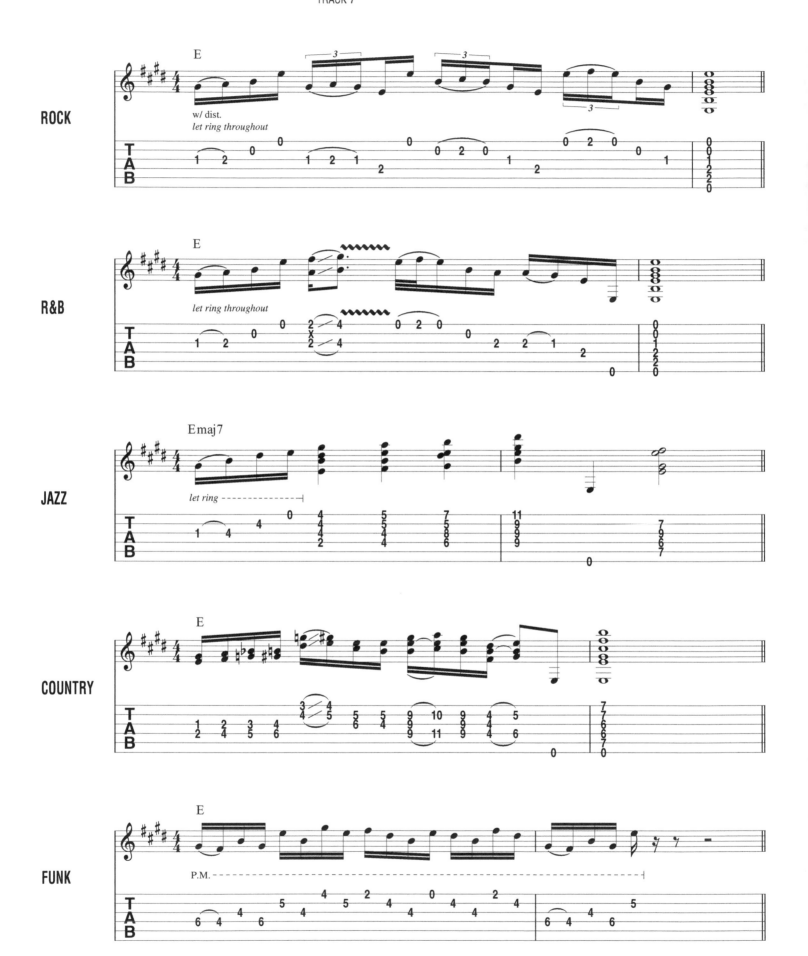

RIFF 8

TRACK 8

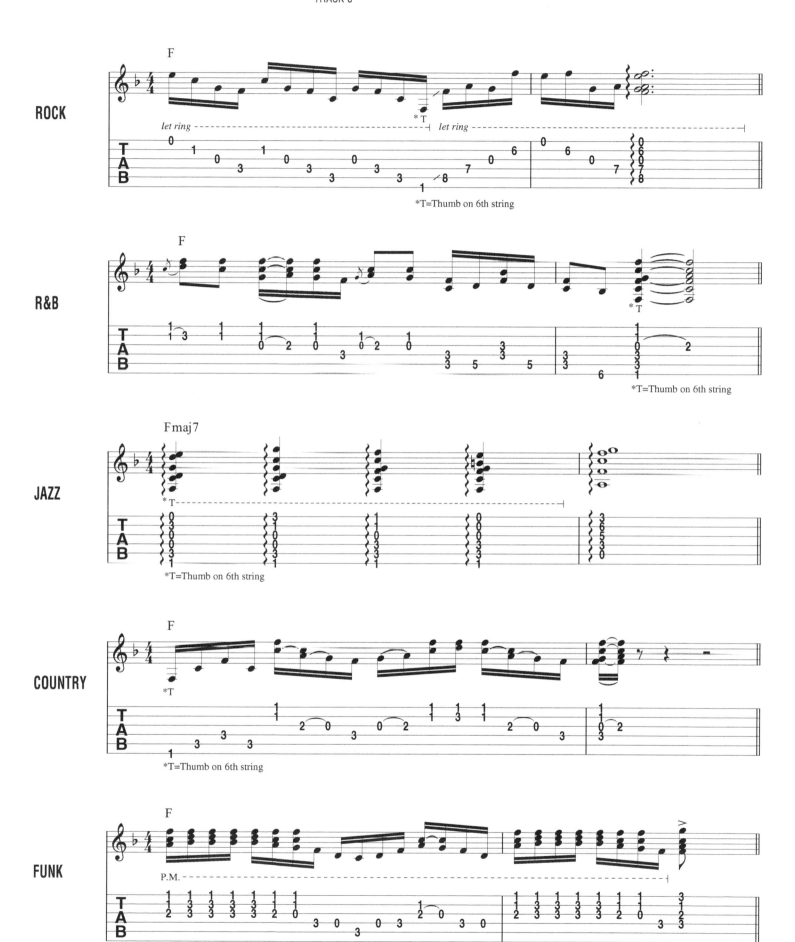

ROCK

let ring — — — — — — — *let ring* — — — —

*T=Thumb on 6th string

R&B

*T=Thumb on 6th string

JAZZ

*T=Thumb on 6th string

COUNTRY

*T=Thumb on 6th string

FUNK

P.M. — — — — — — — —

RIFF 9

TRACK 9

RIFF 10

TRACK 10

ROCK

R&B

JAZZ

COUNTRY

FUNK

 **RIFF 11**

TRACK 11

RIFF 12

TRACK 12

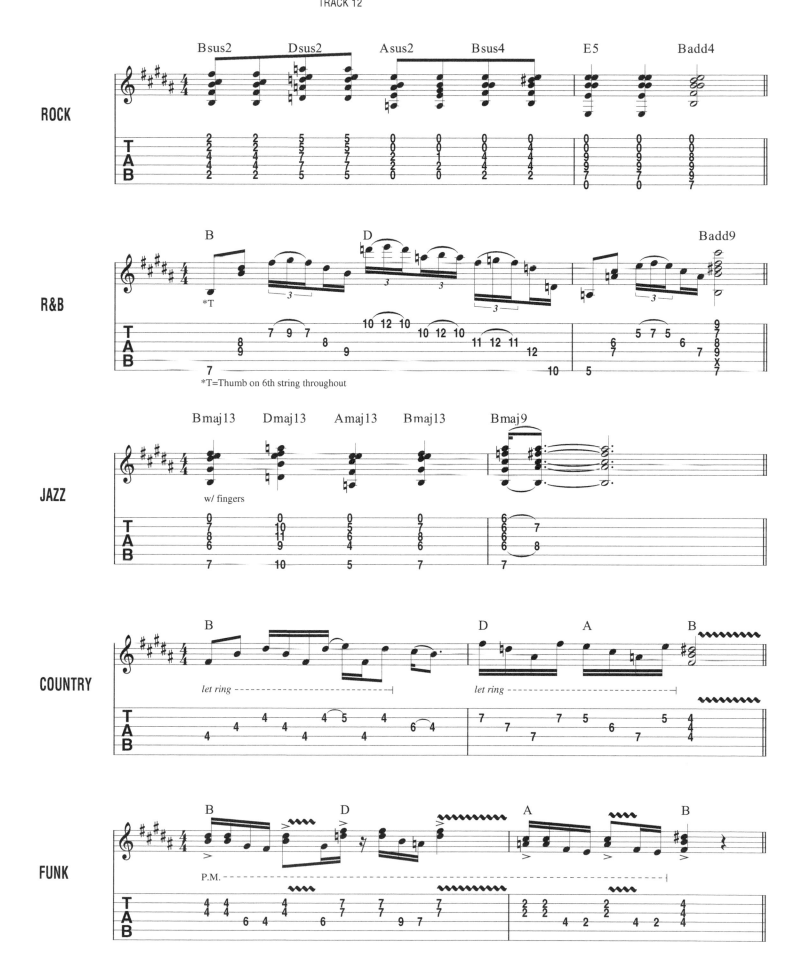

RIFF 13

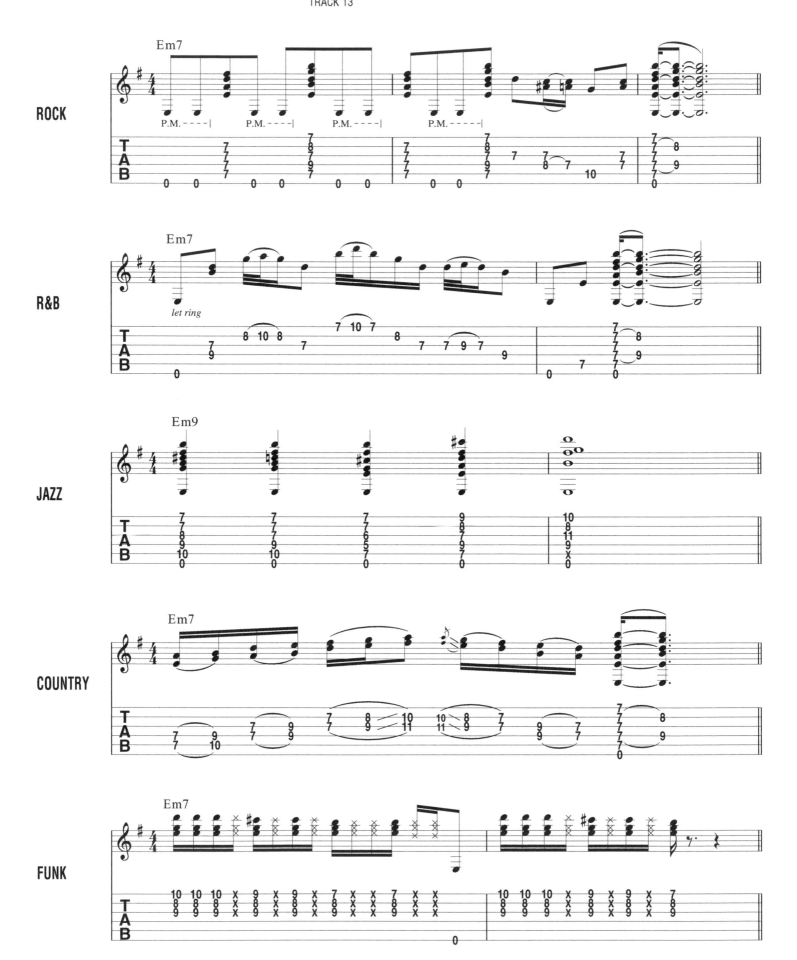

RIFF 14

TRACK 14

FOLK/ROCK

BLUES

JAZZ

COUNTRY

FUNK

RIFF 15

TRACK 15

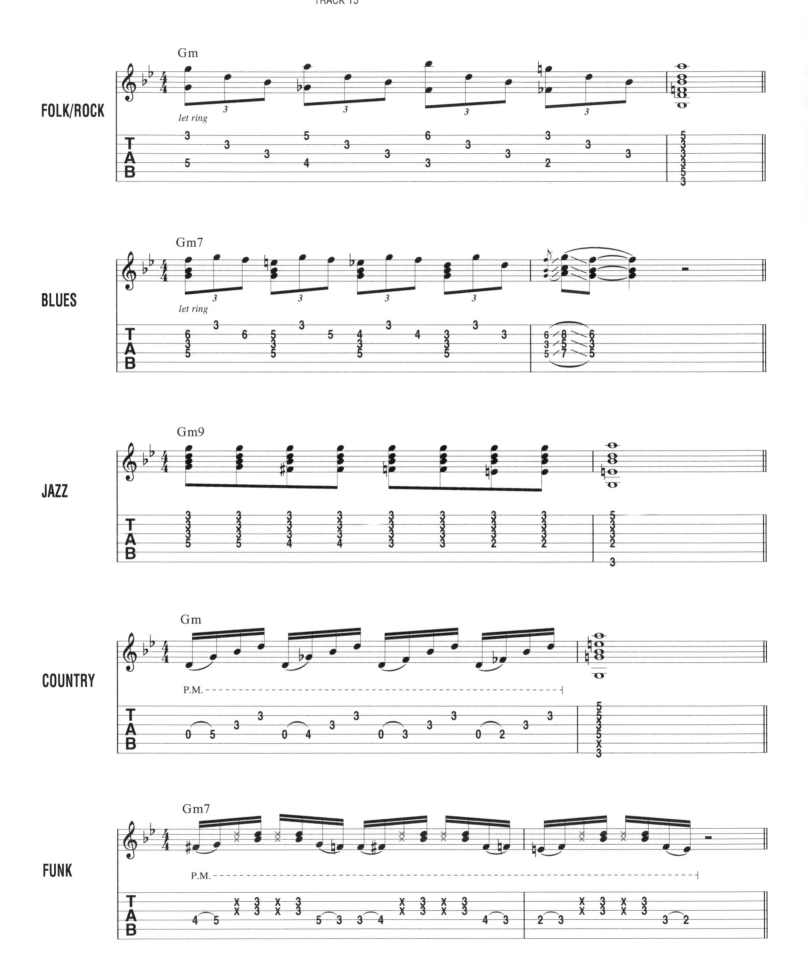

FOLK/ROCK

BLUES

JAZZ

COUNTRY

FUNK

RIFF 16

TRACK 16

ROCK

*Harm. on strings 1-3 only.

BLUES

JAZZ

COUNTRY

FUNK

RIFF 17
TRACK 17

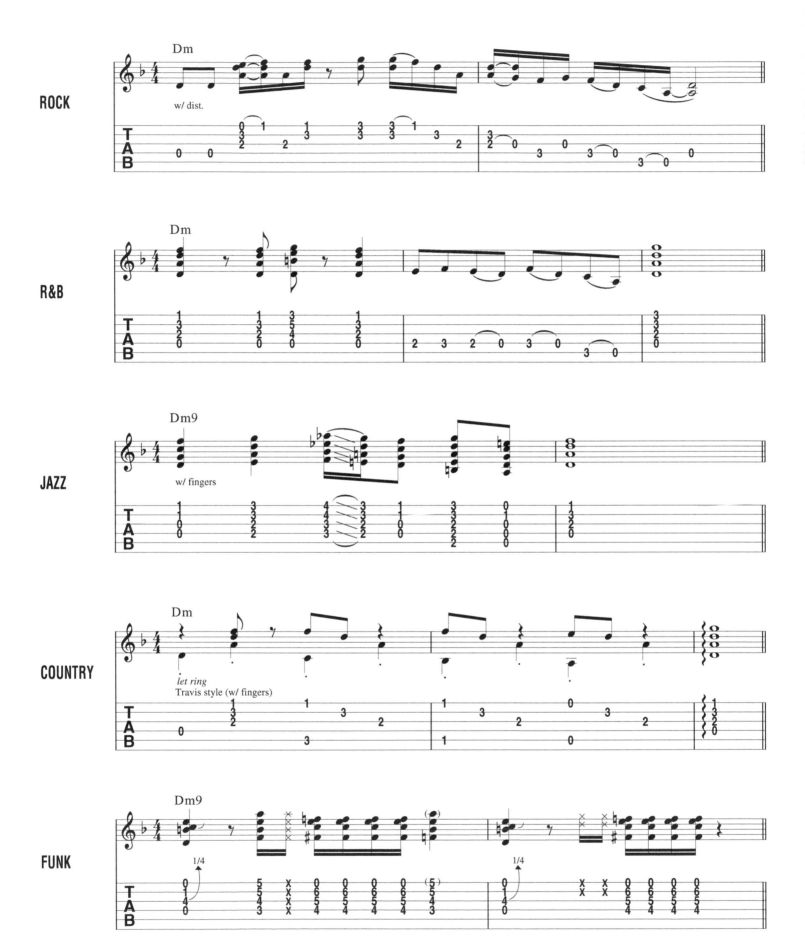

ROCK

R&B

JAZZ

COUNTRY

FUNK

RIFF 19

TRACK 19

ROCK

BLUES

JAZZ

COUNTRY

FUNK

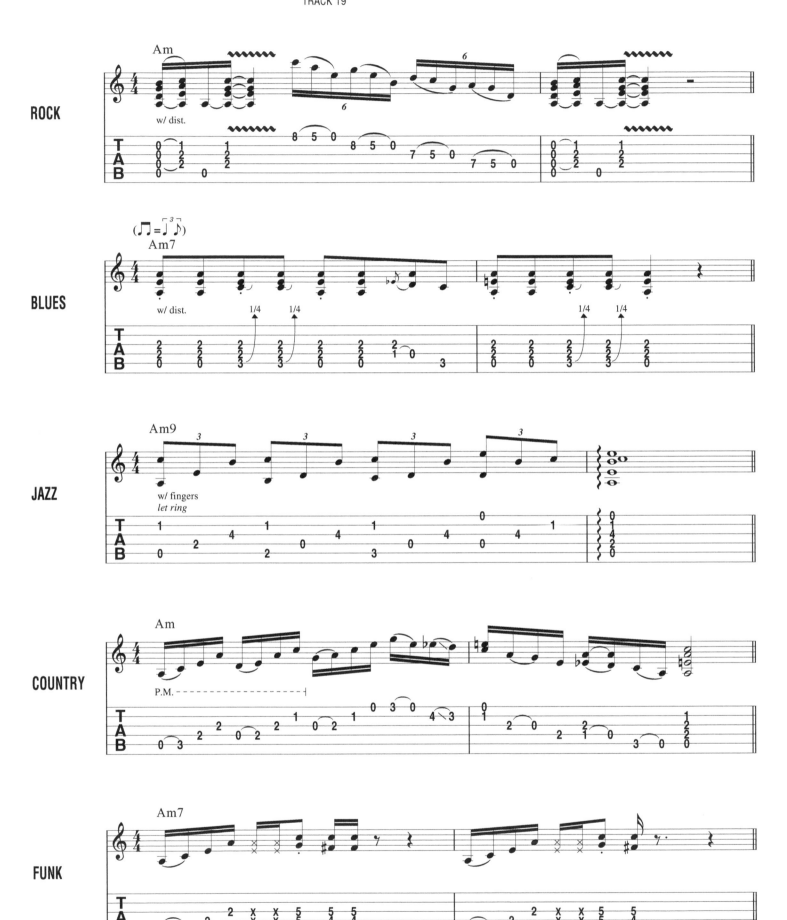

RIFF 20

TRACK 20

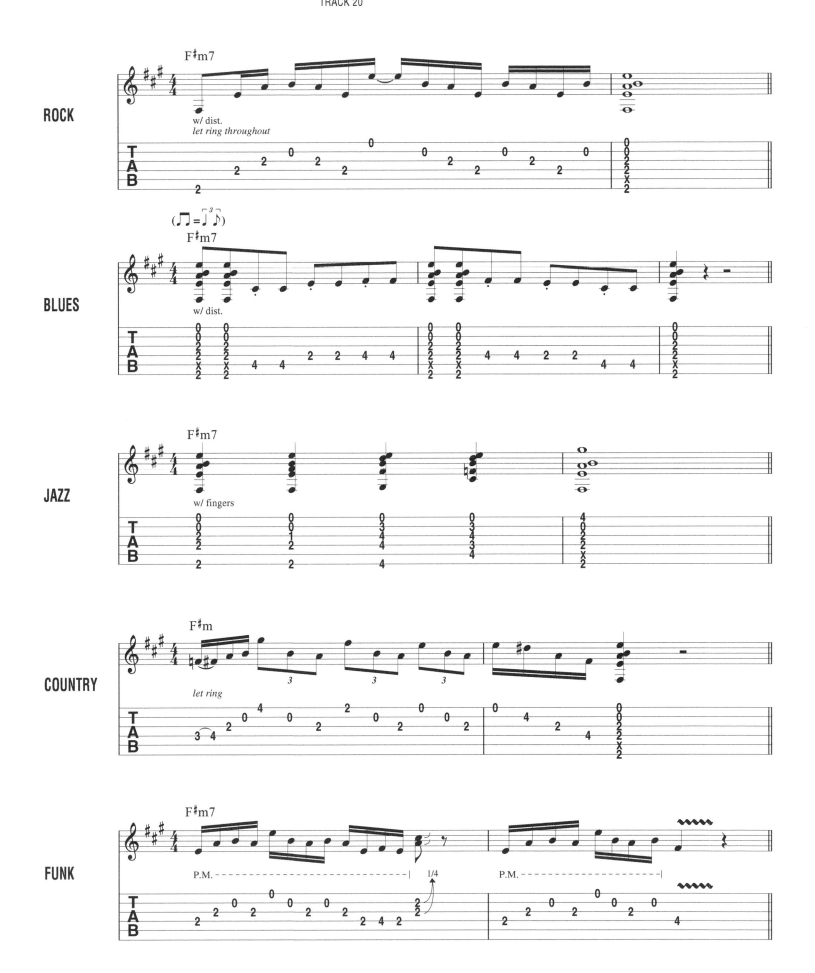

ROCK

BLUES

JAZZ

COUNTRY

FUNK

RIFF 21

TRACK 21

ROCK

R&B

JAZZ

COUNTRY

FUNK

RIFF 22

TRACK 22

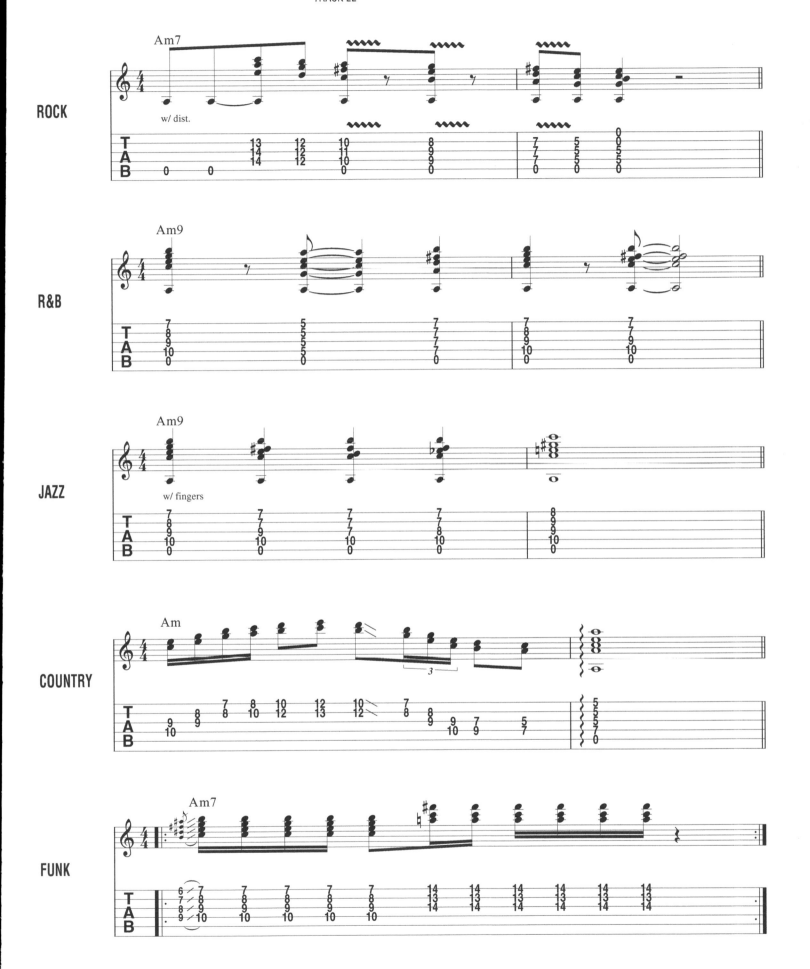

ROCK

R&B

JAZZ

COUNTRY

FUNK

 **RIFF 23**

TRACK 23

ROCK

BLUES

JAZZ

COUNTRY

FUNK

RIFF 24

TRACK 24

ROCK

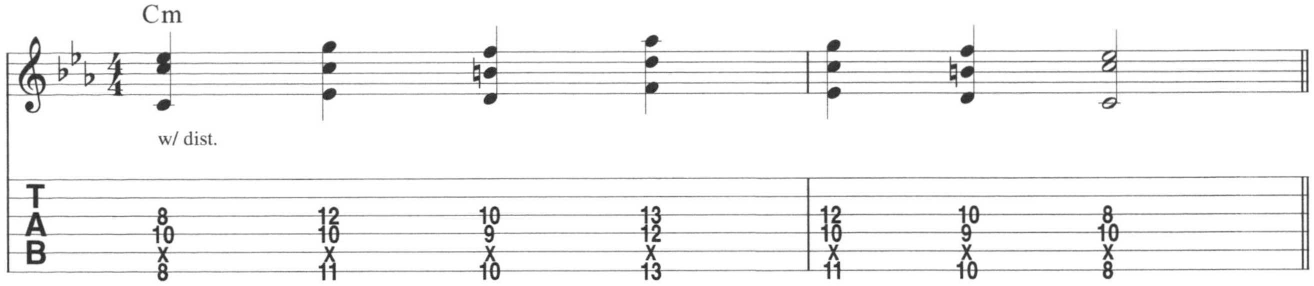

BLUES

JAZZ

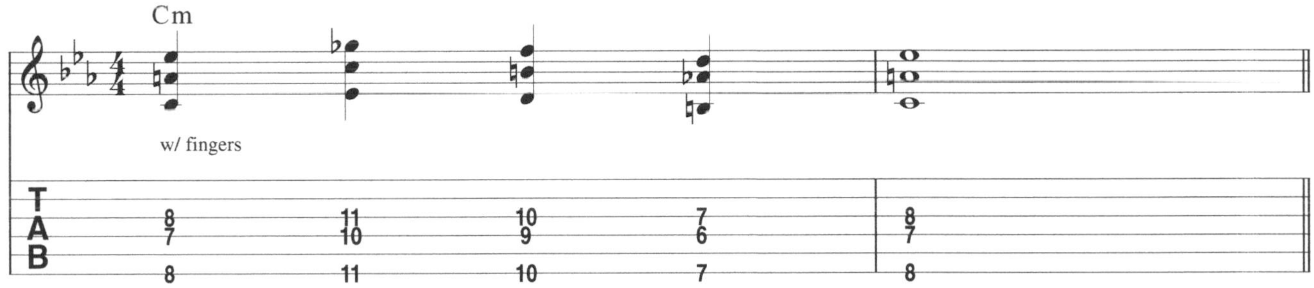

COUNTRY

FUNK

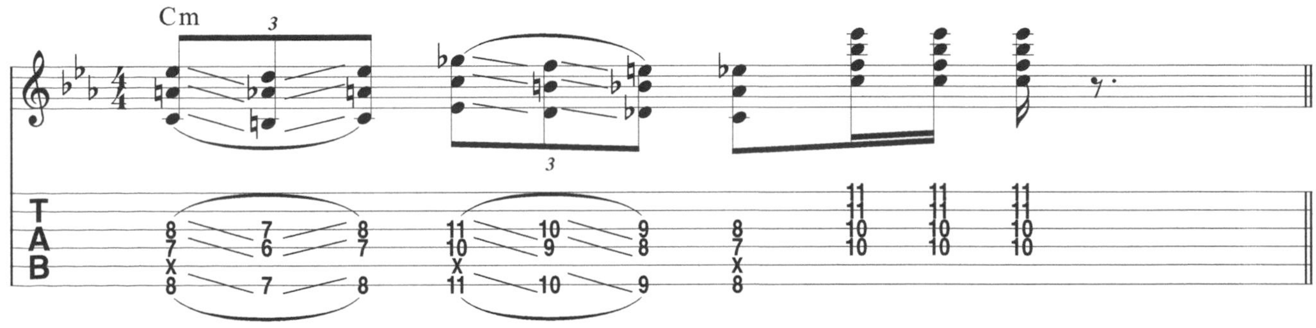

27

RIFF 25

ROCK

BLUES

JAZZ

COUNTRY

FUNK

RIFF 26

TRACK 26

ROCK

BLUES

JAZZ

COUNTRY

FUNK

RIFF 27

ROCK

BLUES

JAZZ

COUNTRY

FUNK

RIFF 28

TRACK 28

RIFF 29

TRACK 29

ROCK

BLUES

JAZZ

COUNTRY

FUNK

RIFF 30

TRACK 30

ROCK

BLUES

JAZZ

COUNTRY

FUNK

RIFF 31

ROCK

BLUES

JAZZ

COUNTRY

FUNK

RIFF 33

TRACK 33

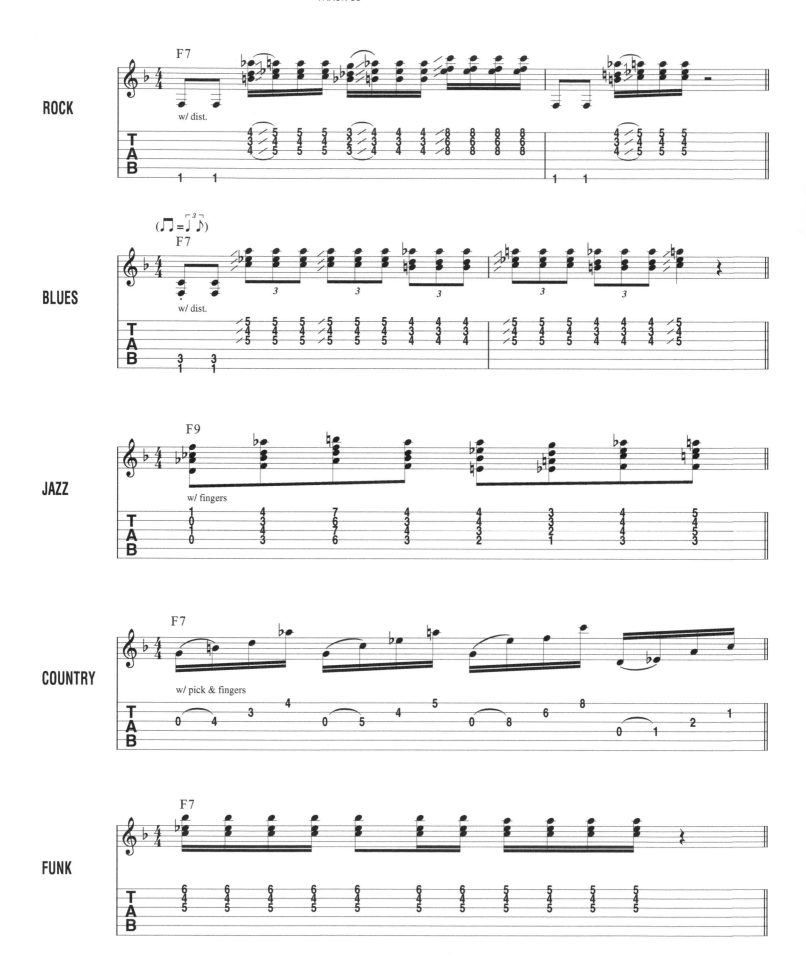

ROCK

BLUES

JAZZ

COUNTRY

FUNK

ROCK

BLUES

JAZZ

COUNTRY

FUNK

RIFF 35

TRACK 35

ROCK

BLUES

JAZZ

COUNTRY

FUNK

RIFF 36

TRACK 36

ROCK

BLUES

JAZZ

COUNTRY

FUNK

ROCK 'N' ROLL #1

TRACK 37

ROCK 'N' ROLL #2

TRACK 38

BLUES #1

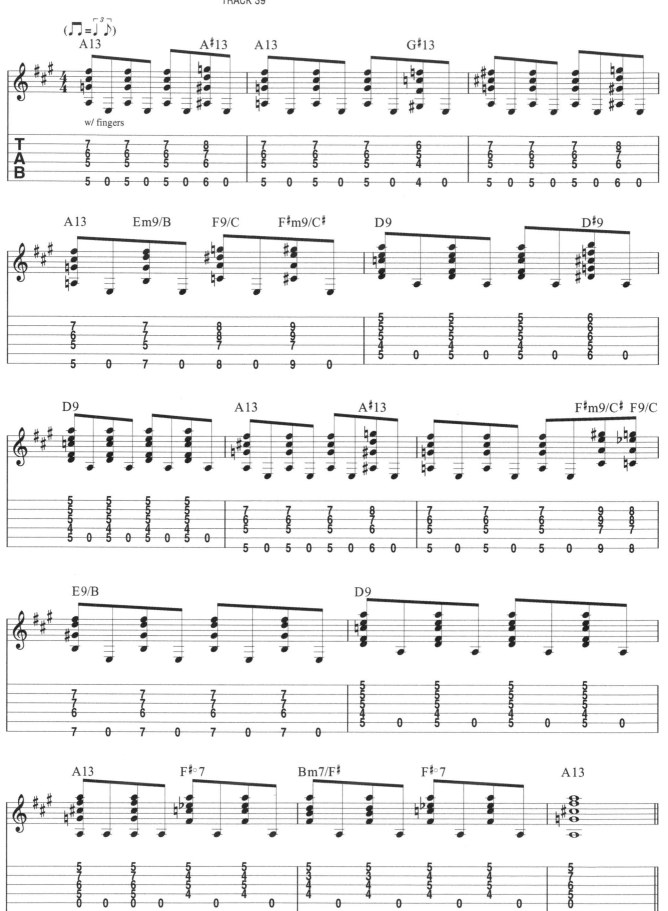

BLUES #2

TRACK 40

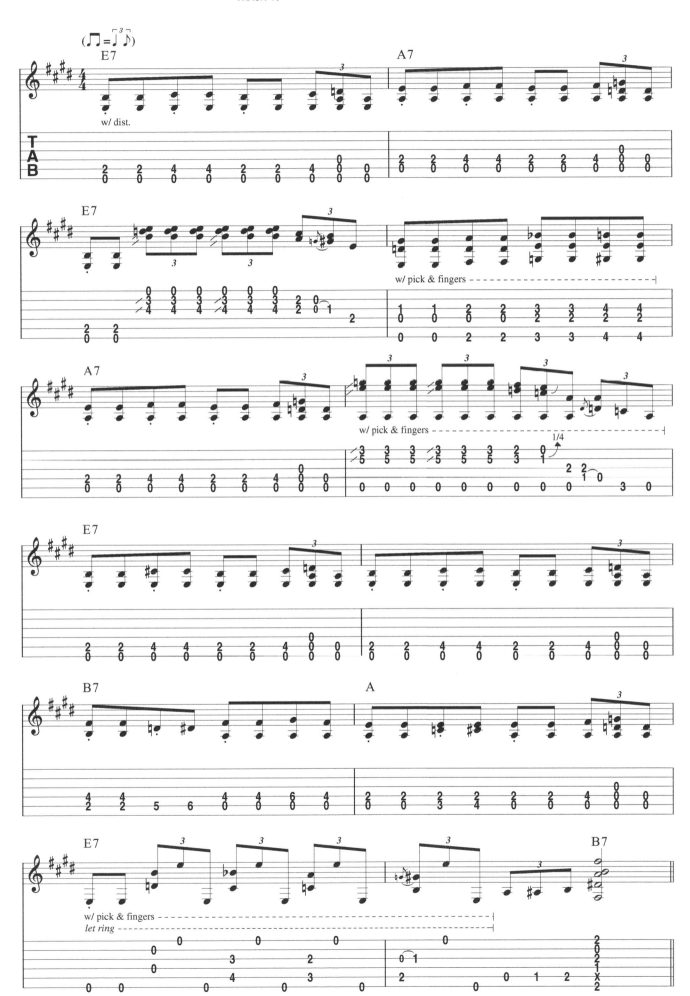

JAZZ

TRACK 41

*T=Thumb on 6th string

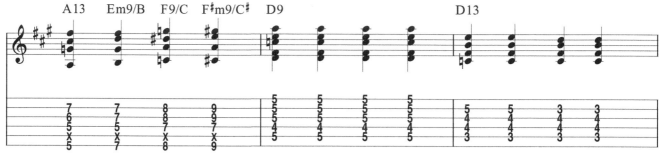

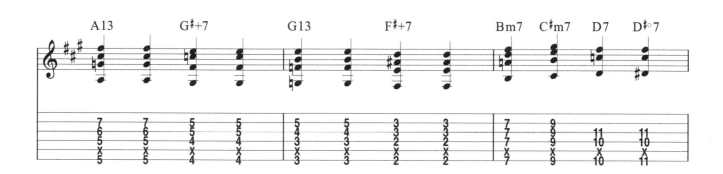

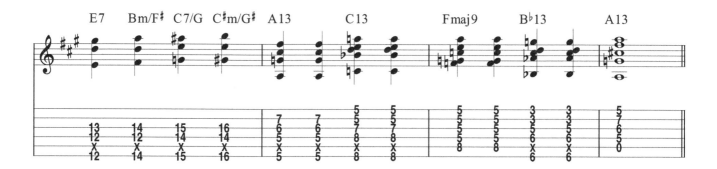

COUNTRY #1

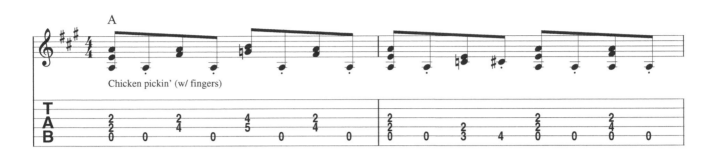

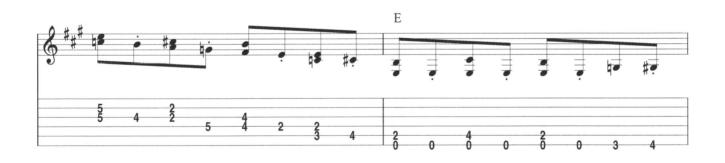

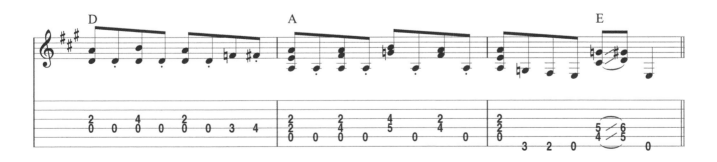

COUNTRY #2

Travis style (w/ fingers)

FUNK

TRACK 44

HAL LEONARD GUITAR METHOD

METHOD BOOKS, SONGBOOKS AND REFERENCE BOOKS

THE HAL LEONARD GUITAR METHOD is designed for anyone just learning to play acoustic or electric guitar. It is based on years of teaching guitar students of all ages, and it also reflects some of the best guitar teaching ideas from around the world. This comprehensive method includes: A learning sequence carefully paced with clear instructions; popular songs which increase the incentive to learn to play; versatility – can be used as self-instruction or with a teacher; audio accompaniments so that students have fun and sound great while practicing.

BOOK 1
00699010	Book Only	$8.99
00699027	Book/Online Audio	$12.99
00697341	Book/Online Audio + DVD	$24.99
00697318	DVD Only	$19.99
00155480	Deluxe Beginner Edition (Book, CD, DVD, Online Audio/Video & Chord Poster)	$19.99

COMPLETE (BOOKS 1, 2 & 3)
00699040	Book Only	$16.99
00697342	Book/Online Audio	$24.99

BOOK 2
00699020	Book Only	$8.99
00697313	Book/Online Audio	$12.99

BOOK 3
00699030	Book Only	$8.99
00697316	Book/Online Audio	$12.99

Prices, contents and availability subject to change without notice.

STYLISTIC METHODS

ACOUSTIC GUITAR
00697347	Method Book/Online Audio	$17.99
00237969	Songbook/Online Audio	$16.99

BLUEGRASS GUITAR
00697405	Method Book/Online Audio	$16.99

BLUES GUITAR
00697326	Method Book/Online Audio (9" x 12")	$16.99
00697344	Method Book/Online Audio (6" x 9")	$15.99
00697385	Songbook/Online Audio (9" x 12")	$14.99
00248636	Kids Method Book/Online Audio	$12.99

BRAZILIAN GUITAR
00697415	Method Book/Online Audio	$17.99

CHRISTIAN GUITAR
00695947	Method Book/Online Audio	$16.99
00697408	Songbook/CD Pack	$14.99

CLASSICAL GUITAR
00697376	Method Book/Online Audio	$15.99

COUNTRY GUITAR
00697337	Method Book/Online Audio	$22.99
00697400	Songbook/Online Audio	$19.99

FINGERSTYLE GUITAR
00697378	Method Book/Online Audio	$21.99
00697432	Songbook/Online Audio	$16.99

FLAMENCO GUITAR
00697363	Method Book/Online Audio	$15.99

FOLK GUITAR
00697414	Method Book/Online Audio	$16.99

JAZZ GUITAR
00695359	Book/Online Audio	$22.99
00697386	Songbook/Online Audio	$15.99

JAZZ-ROCK FUSION
00697387	Book/Online Audio	$24.99

R&B GUITAR
00697356	Book/Online Audio	$19.99
00697433	Songbook/CD Pack	$14.99

ROCK GUITAR
00697319	Book/Online Audio	$16.99
00697383	Songbook/Online Audio	$16.99

ROCKABILLY GUITAR
00697407	Book/Online Audio	$16.99

OTHER METHOD BOOKS

BARITONE GUITAR METHOD
00242055	Book/Online Audio	$12.99

GUITAR FOR KIDS
00865003	Method Book 1/Online Audio	$12.99
00697402	Songbook/Online Audio	$9.99
00128437	Method Book 2/Online Audio	$12.99

MUSIC THEORY FOR GUITARISTS
00695790	Book/Online Audio	$19.99

TENOR GUITAR METHOD
00148330	Book/Online Audio	$12.99

12-STRING GUITAR METHOD
00249528	Book/Online Audio	$19.99

METHOD SUPPLEMENTS

ARPEGGIO FINDER
00697352	6" x 9" Edition	$6.99
00697351	9" x 12" Edition	$9.99

BARRE CHORDS
00697406	Book/Online Audio	$14.99

CHORD, SCALE & ARPEGGIO FINDER
00697410	Book Only	$19.99

GUITAR TECHNIQUES
00697389	Book/Online Audio	$16.99

INCREDIBLE CHORD FINDER
00697200	6" x 9" Edition	$7.99
00697208	9" x 12" Edition	$7.99

INCREDIBLE SCALE FINDER
00695568	6" x 9" Edition	$9.99
00695490	9" x 12" Edition	$9.99

LEAD LICKS
00697345	Book/Online Audio	$10.99

RHYTHM RIFFS
00697346	Book/Online Audio	$14.99

SONGBOOKS

CLASSICAL GUITAR PIECES
00697388	Book/Online Audio	$9.99

EASY POP MELODIES
00697281	Book Only	$7.99
00697440	Book/Online Audio	$14.99

(MORE) EASY POP MELODIES
00697280	Book Only	$6.99
00697269	Book/Online Audio	$14.99

(EVEN MORE) EASY POP MELODIES
00699154	Book Only	$6.99
00697439	Book/Online Audio	$14.99

EASY POP RHYTHMS
00697336	Book Only	$7.99
00697441	Book/Online Audio	$14.99

(MORE) EASY POP RHYTHMS
00697338	Book Only	$7.99
00697322	Book/Online Audio	$14.99

(EVEN MORE) EASY POP RHYTHMS
00697340	Book Only	$7.99
00697323	Book/Online Audio	$14.99

EASY POP CHRISTMAS MELODIES
00697417	Book Only	$9.99
00697416	Book/Online Audio	$14.99

EASY POP CHRISTMAS RHYTHMS
00278177	Book Only	$6.99
00278175	Book/Online Audio	$14.99

EASY SOLO GUITAR PIECES
00110407	Book Only	$9.99

REFERENCE

GUITAR PRACTICE PLANNER
00697401	Book Only	$5.99

GUITAR SETUP & MAINTENANCE
00697427	6" x 9" Edition	$14.99
00697421	9" x 12" Edition	$12.99

For more info, songlists, or to purchase these and more books from your favorite music retailer, go to

halleonard.com

HAL•LEONARD®